Too Close

Ann Alexander

Published by Ward Wood Publishing
6 The Drive
Golders Green
London NW11 9SR
www.wardwoodpublishing.co.uk

The right of Ann Alexander to be identified as author of this work has been asserted by her in accordance with the Copyright, Designs and Patent Act, 1988. Copyright © 2010 Ann Alexander
ISBN: 978-0-9566602-1-3
British Library Cataloguing in Publication Data. A CIP record for this book can be obtained from the British Library.

All rights reserved. No part of this publication may be reproduced, stored in a retrieval system, or transmitted in any form or by any means, electronic, mechanical, photocopying, recording or otherwise without the prior written permission of the publishers. This book may not be lent, hired out, resold or otherwise disposed of by way of trade in any form of binding or cover other than that in which it is published, without the prior consent of the publishers.

Designed and typeset in Palatino Linotype
by Ward Wood Publishing.
Cover design by Mike Fortune-Wood
from original artwork: Lioness by Vaclav Zilvar,
supplied by agency: Dreamstime.com
Printed and bound in Great Britain by
MPG Biddles Ltd, King's Lynn, Norfolk.

For my sister, with love

Acknowledgements

Too close won first prize in **Mslexia** poetry competition, 2007.
On the importance of locks won first prize in **Bedford Open** poetry competition, 2007.
The night we went to Memphis, by way of Solihull won fourth prize, **Peterloo** competition, 2008.
No joke, growing old was published in **Cracking On, (anthology) Grey Hen Press 2008.**

Other poems in this collection have appeared in literary magazines including **Acumen, The Interpreter's House, Magma, Mslexia, Scryfa, Artemis, The Frogmore Papers** and **Openings** and on blogs and websites all over the place.

Contents

Too close	9
A gardener makes love	10
Turning the hard ground	11
Rain coming	12
Half life	13
Found it	14
When the rot set in	15
Lost men, found poem	16
Warming to him	17
The daughter from America	18
Someone else's things	19
Desperate for rain	20
No joke, growing old	21
Mixed bout in a Cornish ward	22
Not safe with husbands	23
The polio pond	24
Growing old is like going to North Korea	25
The grape and the grain	26
The night we went to Memphis, by way of Solihull	27
Fishing	28
On the importance of locks	29
Shock and awe	30
Birth	31
Come clean	32
How we never quite climbed Great Gable	33
Elementary	34
Cabbage cutters wanted. Basic English. Night or Day.	35
Saturday night	36
The tomb of the unknown worker	37
On being asked to plan my funeral	38
Ray lights a fire	39

Fantasy and Reality read a book	40
The party, let it be over	41
Requiem for the terminally unprepared	42
The scaffolders	43
Remembering the Dal Lake, in the rain	44
Loving a married man – the small print	45
Every time I write 'dog' I really mean 'love'	46
The incident	47
Hospital bed	48
Abandoned mine, Dolcoath	49
The things I learnt in the heritage village	50
Last meal	51
Up-country on the train	52
Washing my grandmother's hair	53
On safari	54
Things to make and do with a plastic bag	55
There has to be winter	56
Downsizing	57
Separation	58
Life has become a long wait in a hospital corridor	59
Suicide Grannie	60
Men of enormous power	61
Even though I know there are no wolves	62
Death is a big word	63

Too Close

Too close

On the pillow to my right, the Scottish vicar's wife,
still snoring. I observe, with tenderness,
her open mouth, spread hair.

On the pillow to my left, the conker face
of Ed the vagrant. He's so deep in drugs
he seldom surfaces. The kind you might ignore
on some park bench, attended by an optimistic dog.
Who tends his dog?
I could reach out and touch him, but I won't.

We are too close. All of us
have seen and heard each other doing, saying things
that should be done and said behind closed doors.
We know each other's secrets.
We have witnessed all those small and sharp
unkindnesses that nurses bring.

They know me, in and out. Likewise,
I know his date of birth, his state of mind
- the doctors here discuss it every day.
I know her age, the problems with her kids.
I know her desperation: Edinburgh vowels
aching to be understood in this broad Cornish place.

We have been levelled, me, him, her;
scared, scarred, trapped in the same boat.
His bed's his world. Her world's 500 miles away.
My world comes visiting at noon, tears in his eyes.

A gardener makes love

His gifts: plump carrots, whiskery parsnips,
blue veined cabbages, hearts tight as hazel nuts.
He was not a subtle man.

Not for him the manicured parterre,
the bower, dripping with roses.
He came to me with dirty hands.

His voice seeded love among the rows
of sprouting broccoli. We lay on a bed
of strawberry leaves, two peaches in the sun.

His love, he said, would grow -
not as ivy grows, bending the slender tree,
but like the olive; slow, productive.

We would be broad beans together,
snug in our downy bed.
He offered me an apple, and I ate.

Turning the hard ground

A back of the hand man, this.
He had survived a childhood Sunday stern,
as wrapped about with rules as Leviticus.
And so no kisses, no kind words for us.

The dog fared worse - never walked,
no, not once. Paced the bare yard,
strapped if he did wrong.
I hear him yelping now.

Sometimes he broke out, raced
the Bowjey like a thrown stick.
Once he came home ripped:
my father held a needle in a flame,
stitched his white hide.
The dog lay still as a pool.

Years later, I came back from school
to a quiet house.
The dog was nowhere. In the yard,
a man I did not recognise
turned the hard ground,
tears raining down.

Rain coming

Out in *The Mermaid*, off Land's End,
dangling for mackerel, squinting for shark,
my son turns and says, in a small, dry voice -

Rain coming.

We stretch our eyes for a long, dumb moment
over the waves which are darkening, swelling -
at rain, in a blue-black wall of wet,
massed at the eye's far reach, and closing.

And our boat, which is all about pleasure and sport,
turns tail and runs, like a child in trouble,
rocking and skittering back to the land.

We damn near make it. There's the harbour,
spreading its arms. We fling ourselves at it,
too late. The rain comes swaggering, roaring,
over the sea like a pantomime pirate,
people shouting *Behind you! Behind you!*

Umbrellas flapping, arms alarming,
skipper cussing, the engines coughing,
passengers panicking, heaving, baling,
all so wet we might have been drowning -

without knowing why, we're out and scrambling
back in our element, running for cover.
The wet, white face of my son, eyes staring,
is mouthing over and over,

Rain come.

Half life

The half-grown girl with the small bag packed
and the five pound note and the half-baked plan
plots her escape: at half past ten
when they're all asleep, I'll do it then -

        and is discovered, stopped.

Seventeen, and the bag still packed,
and the fitful sleep on the false friend's floor,
and the slow slip-slide to the faithless man.
And the running away to the rented flat
and the running away from even that,
and the running back from city to town
and town to village and back again,
where the clueless girl with the half-packed bag
and the ten pound note and the half-baked plan
and the new wrong man, plots her escape.

And is discovered. Stopped.

Found it

I was unblocking the drain
with a shovel and a shove and a bucket of bleach
when I rediscovered my feminine side.

I remember the day I lost it,
after the birth of my second child
and before my first divorce.

My children ached to see it,
but it ran from us like money and love -
though sometimes we caught a glimpse.

And now it's back. Dated, dented,
dusty, doleful, demanding, distracted,
and definitely female.

I am old now and have no more use for it.
I am old and cannot afford the upkeep.
I will give it to my daughter. She will know
exactly what to do with it.

When the rot set in

Four drinks on, and he's off.
If only the Bastard hadn't come -

Back to the wall,
straining to hear above the din
of fifty drinkers having fun,
I learn about the bastard Norman earl
who thumped the Anglo-Saxons,
way back then.

If only that so-called Conqueror
had not come over with
his band of mercenaries, he froths,
draining his gin, *we'd all be fine.*

Another sings a different song.
Blame the Empire
and its aftermath, more like -
that's where it all went wrong.

Escaping to the kitchen for some wine,
my plate piled high with Thai,
I overhear my Cornish friend
who's also holding forth.

If only they hadn't come,
she rages to her ancient aunt,
three times gazumped.
If only those bloody incomers
would stay where they belong!

Lost men, found poem

I am ready. I'm ready Warden.
Lord Jesus Christ, I commend myself to you.

That's what counts in the end,
where you stand with Almighty God.

The act I committed to put me here
was not just heinous, it was senseless.

I am not going to struggle physically.
I am not going to shout, or make idle threats.

Peace.

No-one gets closure. No-one walks away victorious.
I am sorry for all the grief I have caused.

I hope you will find it in your heart
to forgive me as I have forgiven you.

Give me my rights. Give me my rights.
Give me my life back.

I am sorry. I have always been sorry.
All right, Warden, let's give them what they want.

From the recorded last words of ten of the 376 prisoners executed in the State of Texas between 1982 and 2008

Warming to him

You'll find him at the gruff and blokey end
of male, grime beneath his nails. He's made
from sinew, semen, grease and grout.

He has the skills you never thought you'd need.
So what if he can't write a letter, won't be taught?
Ask him nicely and he'll kill a rat,

show you how to ride a stallion bareback.
Watch him touch a worn out engine -
Lo! It starts. Can you do that? He sparks

a fire without a match. He will not read.
Trouble parts before him, like the Red Sea waves.
He likes his music loud and leather clad.

Seldom washes, hardly ever shaves.
His favourite food is fresh caught, bloody, hot.
He's been out of fashion, out of luck.

But now a new day dawns. He wakes,
peers through the window at the driving rain,
and rises with the waters. Welcome back.

The daughter from America

flies home to watch her mother die.
Hi mom, look, it's me, your daughter, me -

Her voice strides confidently
round the trauma ward,
a Yankee-doodle-dandy Cornish girl.

There are worse places to die,
and ancient Lizzie Annie rides the thermals
of the finest pharmaceuticals.
Still her cloudy eyes flick flick
from face to face, uncomprehending.

It's your daughter, mom, come all this way -
The neon stranger in the corner
rattles words like pills.

Lizzie Annie, on the final lap
of her long journey home,
cries out, flutters the sheets.

And suddenly the daughter's heart is back
on Helston's granite streets.
She grips her mother's hands
as if to hold her to the world,

cries *dear of her*, crumpling,
finding the proper words at last.

Dear of her is a Cornish phrase meaning *Bless her*

Someone else's things

I like using other people's things,
she said, as we wandered round
the charity shop she called a thrift shop,
fingering this and that.

It means they've been broken in.
I get the pleasure.
Some other donkey's done the donkey work.

Back at my place
we sipped wine from the new
charity shop glasses
and watched the bargain DVD.

She sat on the floor barefoot;
leant towards my husband, looking up
with a face full of smiles.

Desperate for rain

She feels her way back to me
down the telephone line.
I picture her, turning her face to the light
as she squints at the square of sky.
Whatever the outlook, she'll say

> *We're desperate for rain.*
> *Why don't you come home?*

We talk of the weather, my mother and I.
The future is cloudy, the past stormy,
the weather is always safe.

> *Come home. We could walk*
> *through the park, to the shops, to the town.*

Her world is a box,
four walls and a window pane.
Long time since she walked through anyone's door.
She is gasping for talk. I mutter some words
about distance and work.

> *We're desperate for rain,*

she says, back forty years,
and walking her Cornish farm.

> *The man on the telly said rain in the west*
> *but it's stifling hot and no sign of it yet.*
> *Why don't you come home?*

No joke, growing old

Funny how we wrinklies shrink into
a cartoon version of ourselves,
grinning and giggling, eyes a pop,
scribble of hair all anyhow or not at all.

Each day a red nose day, although
we hardly know what year it is,
blinking at The Sun.

I say I say I say (cue laughter) hey!
I used to be, I used to know, I used to live -
yeah, right!

Heard the one
about the bandy legged geezers
in their ankle flapping pants
and kipper ties, skidding
on the day's banana skin
from sparrow fart to nighty-night?
Have you seen us oops-a-daisy grannies
daubing lipstick on frayed smiles?
Two sherries and we're tight.

Toodle pip! All a bit of fun.
A target now for every tittering rogue.
A hoot, a scream, a fright.
After lunch the noisy, open-mouthed
post-prandial; then a g&t or two
before we climb the wooden hill
to kip, warbling an antique song.
Too bad we always spoil the joke
by going on too long.

Mixed bout in a Cornish ward

It's like the UN here, says Camborne Chris,
eyeing me and not the slim Ghanaian nurse.

This sets them off. Mad with pain and fear,
Launceston Lucy comes out fighting.

Where you from? She barks, fists up.
Penzance, I say. I duck and dive. She sniffs.

I mean before. Where you really from?
Two local ladies down the orthopaedic end

we know as Hellfire Corner, referee.
Got to stick together, eh? Says one. *We Cornish.*

Do you know Tom Clemo? Lives by you.
Two beds up, and Glasgow man collides

with Edinburgh woman. He backs off, outclassed.
The doctor's fresh from India. No-one dares

to mess with him. *My parents were born close to here,*
I claim, rallying, *but they moved away.*

No one looks convinced. They round on me.
What town? What was your mother's maiden name?

Saved by the bell. Brenda from Basingstoke arrives
to take the centre bed. The ward goes quiet.

A temporary truce.

Not safe with husbands

Feet, pointed and spiked, teeter towards his brogues.
She puffs her pouter chest, leans into his ear,
burbles *corooo corooo.*

She picks, with manicured nails,
a speck of something small, domestic, from his coat.
She hangs upon his words. *My dear….*

Her clear, bright eyes regard him, and he sees
himself reflected in her glass - a hell of a rogue.
He drops his gaze, drinks in

her almost naked breast, as round and soft
as all the love he's owed; aches to rest his head
right there, thinks *what the heck.* Back home,

she strips the trinkets from her neck, and drops them
on the table, with the number and the name,
which she may, or may not. Even now

his face is fading. She preens and pouts. She sleeps
dreamless and deep, her conscience clear.
Nothing serious, after all. Only a game.

The polio pond

Couldn't get there quick enough,
legs pumping bikes
down nettled alleys,
over bomb sites and the dangerous road,
out of the light

and into this cool spinney, where
a pond of standing water waited,
still as a crouched cat.

We'd heard the polio lived here,
biding its time in mottled dark,
belonging to neither day nor night,
nor any certain thing.

That smell. Sharp underbelly stink.
Breath, in gassy bubbles,
pocked the surface, where
a dead bird floated, wings outstretched.
Red ribs of a child's pram, half submerged,
told their tremendous tale.

We threw sticks, threw stones.
Well back, on guard, then inching close,
we stared into its clouded heart,
swore we saw the bloody eye,
the tentacles,
the curled chameleon's tongue.

Growing old is like
going to North Korea

No-one wants to be here, specially me -
nevertheless I am drawn to the border.
And here it is, this place, like a wound.

They don't do fun. No tour bus waits,
with flirty courier; no stops for coffee-in, coffee-out.
Those of us who come this far
must make our own way through.

Here it's all funny peculiar, and no ha-ha.
Forget about visits to vineyards, or nights
of riotous folklorique. No-one will carry my bags.

Inappropriate smiling may be misinterpreted
and is therefore discouraged. Everyone but me
is in charge and in uniform.

I learn the unwritten rules: *respect the ruins;*
study the economy; do not offend the locals -
or you will find yourself on the road to nowhere.

With luck, I will make it to the far plateau.
I might even find myself
grateful to be here at all. Just to look. Just to be.

The grape and the grain

Two ways to oblivion: first, the grape -
fat, wet, full of the warm south,
mouth-rich with the scent of Burgundy, Alsace.
It sings of dancing feet and long years horizontal.
It is a happy seducer, popping its cork at parties,
tickling the tongues of nouveau bridegrooms,
wetting babies heads. The grape bubbles
with news of vintages and nose and bloom.
Stars demand one, peeled.

The grain is northern. Hard and dry.
Fire on cold nights, a wee dram before bed,
it mutters of ruined mothers and sour breath.
Life goes against it. It screws the mouth,
flies out of Glasgow bars, stares into the fire
and wishes things were otherwise.
It tastes of peat or nothing at all,
and is dribbled out in fingers and shorts.
The grain groans of Stalin and Sassenachs
and the general coldness of things.

The grape it is, then.

The night we went to Memphis, by way of Solihull

Mo has the quiff, Mick the eyes,
Mac, a milkman by day, has the sneer -
and Giorgio is the undisputed
King of the Bump and Grind.

It's now or never -
but does anyone in the Solihull heat
of the search for the best-ever Elvis lookalike
have that special something familiar to those
who were ever shook up over cheap music?

The hard headed woman in the front row
can't help falling, but doesn't throw her pants.
It's not the same when you're size 22.

At Heartbreak B & B, close to tears,
Mo, Mick and Mac swear they don't mind,
pack their satin and rhinestone suits
into their blue suede cases - the very same suits

that their wives will later insist
they put on before the bump and grind,
which everyone will get slightly wrong -
except of course for Giorgio,

who is the undisputed King of it.

Fishing

Every morning they watch for her,
the girl like an egret, stepping by
the scummed edge of the sea.

They see her coming from a way off,
and stand beside the fish market
smoking, smirking, waiting.

Marry me, shouts one, who is already married.
I love you, shouts another,
raising a scaly hand to blow a kiss.

They cast their words like nets

and she, beyond reach,
averts her bright eyes, bends her slender neck,
ignores the men and the reeking market.

She could go by some other way, but still
tomorrow finds her once again
drawn to the stones and the men
at the rough edge of the vast and restless sea.

On the importance of locks

A husband might turn up unannounced,
or his wife surprise him, midway through
a private act. A man might find
his identity gone, along with his wealth.
A star might watch herself, exposed
and crucified on the evening news.
A woman might steal another's child.
A man might lose his coat; his wife
might search his pocket for clues, and find
proof of the things she already knows.
Or a man in a safe house lose his life
because of a window that wouldn't close.
Or a prostitute might end her days
curled up in the boot of a punter's Jag.
A nurse might forge an old man's name
on a pile of cheques; the cheques might bounce
when a hacker breaks into her online bank.
A child might steal from his mother's bag
the money she needs to buy his clothes;
a woman might snooze in the afternoon
and neglect to bolt the kitchen door,
a burglar might enter to steal a purse
and bolt with nothing but blood on his hands.

    And every one of them understands
that then and there and for ever more
private things are things of the past,
for everything's out in the open now,
and nothing is secret, and nothing is sure.

Shock and awe

Minding my own, in tune with my old dog,
my child skipping ahead down a bosky lane,
thinking myself a cog in a clockwork land;

when a distant rumble swelled
to a shaking of earth, the trees trembled,
the birds fell silent, the round-eyed child
flew to my hand, the dog crouched low
and growled - and then

>an explosion of red on brown
>as a score of monstrous horses scattered the quiet;
>and a mob of hounds, all tails and noise,
>frightened us down to the brambled ditch
>as the hunt passed. The riders,
>focussed on something distant, russet and small,
>stood high in the saddle, blind to us there.
>The air thickened and stank
>of dung and sweat, and we might have been
>cringing under a landing plane
>so overwhelming the noise. And then -

they were gone, as an arrow streaks from the bow;
and when they had thundered away
the birds began to sing -
and the child let go my hand and scowled at the track
where the dust hung, high as a standing man,
and it was all as before, though not as before.

For the old dog stood four-square in the lane,
and barked - as if in that tumult of hounds
a longing stirred for the day he might have lived,
had only his luck been otherwise,
had he only been differently born.

Birth

Had I been other than human
I might have laid you, as a bird lays its eggs
in a fledged nest, to jostle your way to flight.

Or like a kangaroo, opened my purse of a pouch
for you, as we jack-a-boxed through the years.

I might, like a fish, have spawned you
to take your chance in the shallows. Or like a spider,

swaddled you in silk, to spin out your days
at the edge of the window pane. I might

have stung you into the body of a host,
or, like a worm, split myself in two for you.

I might have left you under a cabbage leaf,
like a yellow bead, to bloom into butter flight;

or slipped you into a honeycomb,
or slipped you out in a jelly of wannabe frogs.

But because I could do no other,
I did it the human way, my very human child -

struggled you into the world
with pain, and love, and hope, and mess, and fear.
So you would be well prepared for what came after.

Come clean

Why don't you just
tell me the truth?

    There was no plot. He was simply in the wrong place
    at the right time. The thing you are looking for
    does not exist. I will never leave my wife.

    There was no plot. She was simply in the right place
    at the wrong time. We will all die one day,
    and most of us will die alone. He is after your money.

    I will never leave my wife. I will not keep your secret.
    She is not the best mother in the world. I took a bribe.
    The cheque is not in the post. There was no plot.

    Your bottom does look big in that. I have done some
    shameful things. You are not as happy as you say you are.
    You are not as successful as you say you are.

    It is a long time since we kissed, but not long enough.
    He is after your money. You are not good in bed.
    You do not look younger than you are. There was no plot.

Thank you for telling me the truth.
Now tell me the real truth.

How we never quite climbed Great Gable

When we dumped the car at Seathwaite,
I carried nothing at all but the clothes on my back
while you, who'd done it before, were ready for anything,
booted and fleeced, impressively zipped -

And I thought, fair's fair, he's a man - let him shoulder
the map, the cash, the compass, the kitchen sink.
It looked like a climb we could do. But then
scrambling alongside Sourmilk Gill, you said
Give me your hand, go slow - and I leant on you.

Crossing Windy Gap, the going grew hard,
the summit always over the next rise.
In the heat of the afternoon sun,
you put down the burdensome pack and said:
We'll never get to the top, the day is too far gone.

And you folded the useless map. And I said
Then here's where we stay,
here's where I've always wanted to be.
And I gave you my hand. And you leant on me.

Elementary

All night, goosing my dreams;
the far off rumble that could be a neighbour, snoring,
the flash that could be a car but isn't, you know it -

Five in the morning. For luck,
a fisherman turns the ring on his finger,
steers back to the shore. On land,
a farmer stirs in his bed,
counts the electric seconds between
the flash and the crash bang wallop.

And I count, too: ten seconds and falling,
the dawn on hold, and everything waiting.

I hear the click click of a girl, speed-walking
from somewhere to somewhere head down,
the roar like a stalker behind her, and closing,
the sky the colour of lemons
and all the gulls squalling.

Six in the morning. I let out the dog,
who is back in a bark. Five seconds, and falling.
I unplug the telephone, telly, make tea,
and wait for this bigger than everything thing -

Then the first spots of rain. It begins.

Cabbage cutters wanted.
Basic English. Night or day.

I am observing how they stand, graphite dark
and neat as knitting in the distant field;
wondering how so many can be so *one*,
and I think - cabbage?

Next time I'm scratching my own patch,
I'm thinking seeds, cabbage - and the men
who come from far away for nothing much,
and find nothing much,
and are out there now, lopping spattered leaves,
slashing at stalks, up to here in mud.

So when I spot some cabbage, unregarded
on the grass shelf, I understand
it's a serious business, and I choose carefully,
as if they were not all the same,
as if they were not the food of last resort.

And now I have chosen. I have carried it home.
I am squeezing the plump heart,
admiring the slick sheen
of the common or garden, astonishing cabbage.
My fingers slip over satin leaves
purple and petrol blue; I note
how the white veins spread from the stalk
into the filigree end of things;
the weighty roundness making me think of
pregnant bellies or severed heads
and how the smell of it isn't of bedsits or hostels,
but open air and desperate men, longing for home.

Saturday night

and the scattered pack shakes off
its sheepish clothing, slickens and preens,
texts itself alive.

Now is the time for flexing of muscles,
fattening of pockets
with cash, with iPods, mobiles, blades.

One by one, these weekend wolves
mark the place where the sum of their parts
comes together, to make an unstoppable whole,

and move as a pack moves, barking a noise
born of vodka and pills and too many hours
staring at death as a game you can win,

which ceases to be known words, becoming a howl,
understood in the forests and plains
a thousand years under the dog-stained soil.

Understood here, too, in the neon heart
of the fitfully sleeping town, where the pack
sniffs out its prey: lone woman, tramp; or best of all

some other pack, straying as now,
by chance or design, over the crack in the stone.
They smell riot, run baying to find each other

and do - by the station, the shelter, the bar;
where, in that suddenly empty place,
like circles like, grinning in time, moving in time,

these midnight marauders, Saturday warriors,
singing their ancient song, shiny with blood.

The tomb of the unknown worker

No eternal flame flickers for me -
I lived by the rules and the clock. A nine-to-fiver,
till I clocked in for my P45.

No gold watch reminds my grey shade
of the empty years emptying the bins.
No blue plaque bears the legend
*Here's where she fiddled her life away
along with her expenses.*

No-one has put a seat in the park
as a pat on the back for the litter I picked.
Tesco has not endowed
a scholarship in my name,
though I sat at that till
through nine different managers.

I was at the blunt edge.
I took my eye off the ball.
I was surplus to requirements.
I ran it up the flagpole, and no-one saluted.
I hit my head on the glass ceiling.
I suffered from
repetitive strain strain strain.
I passed away after being passed over.

When I handed in my notice,
no-one noticed.

After I died of boredom, I buried myself here,
among the roses. No one, so far,
has come to pay their respects.
Do drop by. There's room for us all,
here at Dunslavin,
with its quite nice view of the sea.

On being asked to plan my funeral

No flowers, by request. No hymns, coffins, priests,
weeping or wake, no passing bell.

Instead, Up-Helly-Aa me. If it's not too much to ask,
launch me a Viking longboat,
lay me on silk, then set a fire and float me
into the drowning sun.

Or, if you will, construct a massive book,
(a replica of Johnson's Dictionary perhaps),
hack out the harmless heart, and bury me in that.

Or lay me down on Sunium's marbled steep,
or plant me in a secret grave, among
a terracotta army of my cats.
Failing that, say bye-bye with a bang,
and shoot me from a cannon's mouth.

Bury me where I fall (even if it's in
a stranger's garden, or the middle of the road)
and plant a quince beside my grave,
wild orchids all around.

Oh, and let there be choirs of angels.

Ray lights a fire

We kneel before the widescreen
as the chubby god of nature skills
shows us how to make a fire.

For the hundredth time, we watch
his boy scout fingers
ease apart the whittled bark,

spread it on a fuzz of moss,
which rests upon a bed of twigs
in a clearing in the heart
of the rainforest.

His grubby hands cup the flint,
tease out the spark, tickle the sticks
and answer all our prayers
with the relief of smoke.

We shush the kids. *Watch Ray* we say,
as he boils his pale roots, dining alone,
except for the camera crew.

And (fervently) we hope
that when the promised end arrives
we too will find an angel, just like Ray,
waiting for us here in Camden Town,
armed with a knife and a flint,
and a strong desire to be warm.

Fantasy and Reality read a book

Turn the page. What waits there?
    In the middle of the forest is...

A wolf? A gingerbread house? Robin Hood?
A rude mechanical, braying in the face
of the fairy queen? The road less travelled?
A cherry, hung with snow? A leprechaun?
Teddy Bears' picnic? Or, in a shallow grave,
a body, badly decomposed?
Turn the page.
    ...a child. In her hands she holds ...

- what? A whetted knife? A mutilated Barbie?
Her mother's heart? A snake? A laptop?
A suitcase full of bloodstained cash? An axe?
A poisoned apple? Book of spells?
A little Indian boy? A bow and arrow? Lunch?
    ...a bird.

What kind of bird? Perhaps
a bluebird, raven, albatross, swan?
Puddleduck? Skylark, Crow or Kes?
Jonathan Livingston Seagull? Owl? Fowl?
Croquet Flamingo? Cratchit goose?
Chicken Little or a hawk in the rain?
    It was a common or garden sparrow.

Finish the book.
    The forest has gone. The child has grown.
    The bird has flown.

Only *what if?* remains, stubbornly refusing to die.

The party, let it be over

Never, no more, the reluctant fixing of dates,
the ruinous shopping, the endless list
of mates and must-haves; those we dread,
but owe.

                  Worse still, some other bugger's bash;
the taxi ride through sharp edged neighbourhoods,
arriving late, cleaned out of cash, in a hail
of false hellos, small-talking over Sixties' songs
and hyper carbohydrate. Cheesy Wotsit smile
bared for the kiss, we launch a dozen conversations.
Michael's broke. Spurs won. Jack's dead.

                  Chattering towards pie-eyed, we join
the jammed and sandwiched women; groped
by blokes attempting furtive passes, sideways-scrutinised
by wives, found wanting. All the gatherings
we should by rights have missed
show in our pinched and painted faces.
Semi-pissed,

                  we wheel out all the tired old jokes,
watch our watches, pocket the borrowed fare,
slip slide to freedom via the loo; then taxi home
to the longed for chair, without our reading glasses.
Never again!

                  The phone. A party? *Wonderful.* When?

Requiem for the terminally unprepared

All those who woke this morning and
will not see night, this is for you.

Who slept through alarms, ran out of tea,
crawled back to bed for that extra hour
that became forever - this is for you.

All who left undone those things
they ought to have done,
thinking they'd have a tomorrow
that will never come, for you -

the ones who overwound their clocks,
complaining of Monday or aching knees,
or work, or wives, and found their lives
stopped like the clock in the song;

who paid off debts they need never have paid;
needlessly cut the hedge, or a friend,
or told off a neighbour - for you I toll
this passing bell: ding dong.

Goodbye, all those who failed to tie
the ends of brief, unfinished lives,
who lost the chance to right the wrong,
rewrite the will, come clean, amend.

The scaffolders

Mostly, they're grizzled as badgers,
but this one's young. Seventeen.

At break, he's squashed among them
like a pet pup, head down,
delicately constructing a roll-up,
while they quiz him about girls.

When I bring tea, he's red as a warning flag.
They tell me he would like a job in wildlife.
They laugh, cough, scratch.
Training to be a monkey, like uz.
They keep him in their sights.

At noon, his mother comes
with his forgotten lunch.
She carries the plastic box
to the rooftop where he works, three storeys up.
Shins up ladders and skirts metal poles,
without a *May I*, or the statutory hard hat,
or glancing at the health and safety book
the gaffer carries in his coat.
The grizzlies watch her, store the memory.

Next day, he's late. His mother rings.
A hangover, she says, firmly.
She didn't want to wake him.

Remembering the Dal Lake, in the rain

She settles her woolly bulk
into the corner of his cab, and she instructs:
Solihull Station. Pause. Please.

The traffic light shows red. While they wait,
the driver says (to fill the empty air) -

Not from round here, I don't think?
She smiles. Nor you! Where are you from?

Brum, he answers, then another pause -
but my parents are Kashmiri.

Suddenly both of them are speaking Urdu.

His mouth erupts with words
his mother taught, while the Midlands rain
falls from an industrial sky,
and she feels, on her memory, the touch
of a brown hand.

Aapka naam kya hai?
She tells him her old maiden name
- how she loved her ayah,
longs to see again the land *he's* never visited,
the far, untasted country he calls home.
The light is green.

He takes the tip,
and promises to make that journey home,
to witness for himself the houseboats,
the mountains, the clean, white air;
the beauty of the Dal Lake, in the rain.

Aapka naam kya hai? - What is your name?

Loving a married man - the small print

Sure, give him a ring -
if you're after sex from *cinq a sept*,
a quick coming and clock-watch going,
sometimes not even making it
all the way to the unmade bed.

There'll be no wedding ring for you.
You pray to a god you don't believe
for the rushed call from the end of his road
where you sometimes cruise,
all the aching night,
slow down, speed off, eyes red.

Sure, give him a ring - as the bells ring in
another crushing Christmas Day,
hollowed out holidays, years of it,
nothing to show but tears and texts
you are told to erase, and don't, kept sane
by the treat (or the threat) of a mad weekend
as he lies on the phone, to his wife -

And, years later, to you, too,
with no hard feelings after, right?
And you muse on love which never rang true;
wanting him with you, and wanting him dead;
and longing to bring it crashing down -
that wife, those lies, that life.

Every time I write 'dog'
I really mean 'love'

A dog makes you happy. It is faithful, it is fun.
A dog likes to play, and will lick you all over.
You can go home to a dog at night
and never feel lonely again.

A dog needs you near, all the time.
You have to feed your dog, groom it, walk it,
every single day. A dog is expensive.

If you do not master your dog, the dog will master you.
A dog can live for many years,
which is sometimes much too long.

You can never spend time with another dog,
or your main dog will be jealous, and yap and yap.
A dog is a martyr to parasites.

A dog goes wrong, grows old, and slobbers.
An old dog is not a pretty thing. Sometimes a dog dies
when you least expect it.
You might even want to put the dog to sleep.

Are you sure you want this dog?
Are you *absolutely* sure?

The incident

Before the thing that happened
happened

      and I stood waiting for the 6.15
      that would take me to you
      dressed in my usual
      with my book in my hand
      to finish later that night
      (after we had made love
      which we would surely do
      fired up by a generous g and t
      ice and slice the way I like)

and though I wish I could say I saw it coming
with my famous sixth sense
I had absolutely no hint of an inkling.
However, I *can* honestly say that until then

      I had never felt happier.
      I had never felt more in control.
      Or safer. Or more in love.

Hospital bed

Most of us start our lives on a bed like this -

a mean sized metal machine on skittering wheels,
where thousands of others were born before us
and will be after. And chances are
we were yelling with shock, shouted into the world
and slapped to life, wiped and weighed
and maybe found wanting.

> Then the middle bit:
> learning, belonging, laughing, loving,
> hating, crying, longing, forgetting -

and often found wanting. Chances are
we'll be carried here at the end of it,
weighed and wiped and shocked to life,
before being whispered out of the world
as thousands of others have been before us
and will be after, strapped to
a mean sized metal machine on skittering wheels.

Most of us end our days on a bed like this.

Abandoned mine, Dolcoath

I call him to the edge
but he will not come down.

Though I tell him seven miles of tunnels
fan out like a fossil's spine
he will not come.

He is a surface dweller, player in the sun,
and these are shadows. Old ground.
All that lies there, half a mile deep,
does not concern him, now.

A man could die down there, he says,
walls bleeding rain, the roof space low
enough to make a grown man crawl -

and he won't crawl
where all those nimble Buccas crawled,
knocking after copper, tin,
tapping the flat lode;

feeling their hearts bursting in
their coffin chests, dissolving in
their own sweat, naked and on fire.

Men who never could believe in God
shook at the sound of phantom Knockers,
tapping them to choking death -

daring to do what he will never do.
Although I call him to me, call and call.

The things I learnt
in the heritage village

Crowded in the family's third best car
we head out west, to find out how it was.

For fifteen dollars each, which someone pays,
we're through the turnstile, find ourselves slap bang
in the nineteenth century. There's a man

shoeing a real horse and the real horse farts;
a woman brings his lunch,
packed in a settler basket, cheese and bread.
There are his tow-haired children (five)
trying not to look at us, and in a real log house
a plastic baby, in a wicker basket by the fire.
Further down the main street, kindly Doctor Lewis
organises all his knives, and in the distance, see,
a farmer ploughs the solid field, and in the shop
a grocer, with a chalk and slate, tots up the daily sum.

Suddenly I need the loo.
I find a privy, tucked behind the general store,
and gently push the stencilled wood -

No place to go. No thunder box.
Instead, a list of dos and don'ts.
Do not step out of role. Smoking is forbidden on this site.
On the wall a phone - the direct line to now.
A list of numbers: fire, police.
A poster: *Terrorist Attacks*, in case of.
There's a first aid chest, a box of latex gloves,
and, on a chair, some adult magazines.

On Main Street, a man in clergy clothes
directs me to the twentieth century loo,
tips his hat, bids me have a real nice day.
And winks.

Last meal

There will come a time
when they say in their kindly voices

What would you like for your last meal?
You can have anything, anything at all -

Trembling beneath the shadow
of the metaphorical rope, I will reply:

Best make it chicken –

A chicken's life is short and pointless.
Like me, it spends its little time
pecking its neighbour, scrabbling in the dark,
without a thought for what the dark might be.

They will ask, anxious to please,
Breast or leg? I will reply:
Give me the wishbone, only that -

and I will wish for all of it again,
the short and pointless life,
the neighbours with their claws and beaks
and the unknowable, unimaginable dark.

Up-country on the train

Not just because
the landscape plumps, opening like a fan of notes,
till the green blurts into raw towns and is lost -

Not just the way
the train ups-speed, slamming between walls
loud with the urban shout of the spray can,
air heavy with the odour of sandwiches -

Or the way
voices round me tongue-twist, turn in
on their own vowels, emerge industrial;
one-way chats into cupped hands,
Plymouth...Bristol...running late -

The way faces about me
change from apples to orchids,
ears plugged with muffled drum -
staring blank eyed at houses Legoland-tight,
banked beside rivers of trucks,
and the sky starry with brand names -

It's the way I suddenly feel not much,
out of style and time,
any rubbish bumpkin from any rubbish town.

Washing my grandmother's hair

How like an egg, the ancient head
feathered with its scant braid,
skin shining through
as if she were lit from within.

She'd weathered three score years
and more, past my raw ten;
unbending, straight-backed lady
from a surer century, head bent above
the square stone sink, as I
soaped and tickled, half afraid to touch.

So easily broken - yet so solid sure.
The skin moved loosely back and forth
across the old skull, yet I knew
the will that lived beneath was forged
in wars and hardship, would not break.

Come, dear, and wash my hair -
and I was honoured by the task,
as if she'd given me a robin's egg,
and into my small hands had passed
that fragile treasure, trust.

On safari

Setting out, we ease into adventure with
the twitching of small birds, thrilled
by what's to come. Someone loads
the four-by-four. We think we travel light,
but there's a backup truck behind, before -
we have to sleep somewhere, our bones
too soft for solid ground.

We have to sleep somewhere; tents must be
tough enough to keep out beasts,
the nets above our beds protect us from
the various forms of fly. We have to sleep:
noises all around give sleep the lie.
A water flask contains the single malt
that helps us to forget the lion's roar.

We have to eat. Hampers offer feasts
we might expect in Cheltenham. We dine
off china plates. We wipe our mouths
on travellers' tales. We ought to drive.
We ask for more. Someone loads the gun.
We wish ourselves at home, and yet
we have to drive. We tremble at the thought

of what's to come: the snake, the buffalo,
the spider like a human hand outstretched,
the missing petrol and the stolen food,
the phones that never work, the lion
that even now takes back the jungle night.

Things to make and do with a plastic bag

Hang it from a hawthorn hedge
among the darling buds of May.
Torch it in a wheelie bin on bonfire night.

Mute the silvery throats of swans.
When the sea-turtle hunts for her lunch,
imitate the action of the jellyfish.

Hold the worldly goods of the homeless,
and make a bed for them to lie in
on the wet winter pavements.

Use one to snaggle the teeth of a plough,
to line the nest of a magpie, choke the lark.
Block drains, drift like toxic tumbleweed,

from Mongolia to Maine.
Bling the landfill with a blaze of red and green
where no rose will ever bloom.

Teach a child its letters - and how to shop.
A is for Aldi, Z is for Zara.
Make it last for a thousand years.

What more can we do with this plastic bag?
Has anyone any better ideas?

There has to be winter

Though we might wish it otherwise,
dreaming of Italy in the spring -
there's no escaping this cold northern wind
as our sun dips.

There has to be snow, falling like years -
blank and relentless, all too soon.
There has to be this clearing out
of rusty leaves as our old world departs.

We, who have basked in the sun
so long, must face it now - and are
surprised to find some beauty in it.
Not the pale hope of what lies waiting,
easy balm for optimistic hearts -

but beauty, all the same. This white and fire time,
this time of cracking ice, of endings; loss
come all too soon and all too hard,
however long our lovely autumn days.

And though we say why us, why now?
marvelling at this time
so out of kilter with our simple plans;
we watch with wonder as the winter grips,
cold, magnificent, and pure,
and greater than the sum of all our parts.

Downsizing

Beautiful or Useful? I hold them to the light
and judge - most things here
are one thing or the other, in this home
that never carried ballast.
Sell, give, chuck, burn.

I am shifting. In the dining room
six chairs have disappeared. Useful *and* Beautiful.
Your chair my chair her chair,
with three for all those friendly faces
leaning in for food and wine, and talk.

The table, crumbed and cracked,
has lost its polished function, and become
a shelf for boxes, on and underneath.
No amount of grease,
elbow or otherwise, can cover up
the rings that tell of careless joviality.

Over all, dust. Beneath the sofa,
down the sides of chairs, among the paperclips;
flakes of skin, hair of the dog, testament
to all the years of shedding: skin, dog, things.
Dust. No use, no beauty.
Can't be sold or given, can't be left.

We must take it with us,
before they come with *their* kids, books, lives -
the stuff we're shedding now, without regret,
and feeling all the cleaner for it,
lighter than air, fresh as a washed sheet.

Separation

I was trying to remember
the last time I was happy
and what it felt like
and of course
it was the last time I met you

and only at the very end of the day
as I sat on my train and you on yours
did the tears fall

and kept on falling
as the nights closed in
and the cold and the rain
and the miles between
and me sitting here
trying to remember
the last time I was happy.

Life has become a long wait in a hospital corridor

Flicking through *The Truth About Your Psoriasis*
and - hot off the press -
Boils, Burns, and Sleekit Beasties

I notice how much difference a uniform makes
to a young girl's gravitas

and how, for the sick, when troubles come
they come, like sorrows, not as single spies.

I am wringing my hands in gel as if
praying to the Godliness
that is next to Cleanliness.

Malaria, I learn: *It only takes one bite.*
I muse on the chances of catching it
in West Penwith. Meanwhile,

I am discovering that a two o'clock date
means an afternoon on a stained chair.
Living with Piles and Varicose Veins
seems like a distinct possibility.

I turn to *Hello* for light relief,
wondering who are these unknown stars
with their one-word names, and their wasted faces.

Suicide Grannie

Here come the whisperers:
    Do you *really* want
    on and on and on
    worse and worse
    pain and suffering
    never a hope of

    do you understand what I'm saying, dear?

Now she has agreed to take a trip to paradise
via the plane, the car, the antiseptic flat
overlooking the conniving town;
video explaining why, why now,
smiling watchers daring her to change her mind,
and everyone being nice -

    do you understand what I'm saying?

She has said her obliging goodbyes,
ordered her small world;
she has done the necessary praying
and in spite of it, can't help but feel excited.
She will not need to pack.

    Do you understand?

A moment, all it takes to take the dose,
detonate the righteous anger,
shift the blame, make the headlines,
and at last
feel some kind of control.

Men of enormous power

still creep down narrow stairs to darkened rooms,
to whisper in the ears of shackled men,
who will - eventually - let slip
every truth the world might want to hear;

and women of a certain age still climb
the stairs to lonely beds at four o'clock,
sleep to the radio's whisper, wish themselves
beloved and certain, safe in a just world;

and dogs still sleep the separate hours away
with one ear cocked and ready, for the sound
that doesn't fit the jigsaw of the night,
and might explain the whispers, and the chains;

and are surprised to wake up yet again,
and find the sun still leaking round the blinds,
and loosen their bruised tongues to tell the world
any little thing it wants to hear.

Even though I know
there are no wolves

and though it is bright day,
and I have men around me
that are fat -

even so,
the night is closing in.

The men will soon be gone -
and, look, the path which was so clear
when we left home
is disappearing now into the trees.

Isn't that a wolf, calling?

The feral dogs we always notice
when we walk this way
are coming closer to the path,
and there's a smell that's definitely *wolf*,

although I know there are no wolves
but only these familiar feral dogs,
who roam the bruised, abandoned woods
and howl, like wolves,
under the yellow, closely-watching moon.

Death is a big word

Long and *lingering* are small words.
Kind is a small word, wishing it was a big word.
Cancer is a big word, one of the biggest,
but not as big as *death*.

Medicine is a small word. *Treatment*
is a tiny word, wishing it was a big word.
Hopeless, painful, these are small words.

You always and *You never*
are combinations of small words
which become big when used too often
and said with sufficient force.
See also: *I need you* and *Please don't go*.

If only and *too late* are small words
that become big words when said in a certain way.
Never is a big word. *Love* is a very big word
that will become small when used too often
and said without sufficient force.

Goodbye is a small word,
except when used as a last word.